Letters from the Drinking Town
Gin and Tonics Across Worcester
Volume 2

David Macpherson

Introduction

I think that it is best to be brief here. There is not a lot to say that the body of the essays don't. Let it just be pointed out that I created a project in 2014 where I was to go to every bar or place that had a liquor license in the City of Worcester Massachusetts and have a gin and tonic. The rules were to have that one drink and then leave. I created a blog called Gin and Tonics Across Worcester and I posted what I found.

I did this steadily for 144 bars in 18 months. Then I called it over. But the next year, I started again to fill in the new bars, I did over a dozen and then stopped again. When I started a third time to do this silly task, I was interested in changing up how I was writing about the bars and the act of bar going. I wanted something that wasn't a travelogue of the new bars of Worcester. I wanted tales of a city as told by the bars people drank at. So I started writing them as letters. As drunken dispatches.

This was freeing to me and I was very happy with what I wrote. I knew I was going to gather these "letters" together as a book. But then I ran out of steam. I lost interest in going to new bars. I just didn't have in it me. Also, the extreme acid reflux I had made drinking alcohol a poor choice.

That meant I didn't have enough essays and reviews for a book, even the small one you now have. My solution was to have all sixteen letters and a few other pieces I wrote earlier for this blog. I included three dispatches from my second go-around. If you want to read of the first 144 bars, there is a book out called "Gin and Tonics Across Worcester."

A note on my name. At first, I wanted to be anonymous. I didn't want to have friends worry about my drinking activities. I wanted to go in under the shadow of a fake name. That was why I called myself Dante of Worcester. I thought of this as a tour of hell, or at least drunken heaven, which has many of the characteristics of hell.

The thing was, as I continued to write this blog, I became quite proud of what I produced. I wanted people to know it was me. I held off revealing my name until in one of the letters, when I wrote of Kids and Bars that I figured I must disrobe from the name Dante. It was a personal piece and I felt it would be disingenuous if I signed it with a pen name. For the rest of the letters,

I alternated between Dante and Dave, never sure in who's pen I was scratching out all these words and drinks.

Thanks for deciding to give this collection of bar writings a chance.

David

Letter One - Gin and Tonics at the Ballot Box

Dear Worcester,

Hi Worcester, it's Dante and I am happy to write to you after eight months.

What is it about March that makes me thirsty with curiosity? Three years ago in March of 2014 I started a silly project where I was to go to every bar in Worcester and have a gin and tonic and then write about it. I went to 144 bars in 18 months. This is no world record, but it was fun. Then last March, I got the itch, the urge to check out other bars I had not gotten to. I went to 13 bars in four months. That was fun and I thought it was over and my itch had been scratched but here we are, in March once more. March, time to go out and see bars. Have a gin and tonic and try to live to tell the tale.

I was driving into Worcester today to see a friend, and then to sit down at a coffee shop and write up a report for work and then out of nowhere, I said, "It's time to have a gin and tonic." And like that, I have started up these letters to you. I know of a few new bars, so I will have places to try. The closest place for my needs was The Ballot Box.

The Ballot Box is located at 9-17 Kelley Square. It is where the Greyhound Pub and for a little bit a hot spot called Varsity resided. Even though I went there, I couldn't remember its name and had to check my notes to remember Varsity. Former Sheriff Glodis has now created the Ballot Box. In one of the articles about its opening, Mr. Glodis stated that he wants it to be the Hard Rock Cafe for the political set. I'm sorry, but he should aim higher.

I went in the middle of a Sunday afternoon. Around two. Yes, Worcester, I know that is not the best time to see a bar and get what it is about, but that is the time I had. Also, if a bar is open, it is open. The off hours is a time a bar shows its real face, the time it greets you without its makeup on and wearing only a tattered housecoat.

I went in and there were three or four at the bar and in the second room, at tables there were another ten or twelve or so. Not bad for a cold Sunday. The bartender was good. Friendly. Greeted people when they came in. I got a tall gin and tonic for 6.25. He asked if I wanted a lime. It was fine. Nothing special, but pretty good.

The place is clean and open. The second room is great. It has black leather furniture to sit and move and shake Worcester politics I suppose. Or talk about the Bruins or the Red Sox or why that girl won't call him back. You know, the important inebriate conversations.

The walls are full with wonderful old Campaign Posters. There is an old ballot box on the floor. I spent a good time looking at the posters. They were awesome and worth the time to go and have a beer.

Seeing the posters is like going to an art gallery. Which made me think that what we need is a walking tour of Worcester Bar Art. All the places where you can see interesting art and have a shot of whisky. Ballot Box will be on the tour, as well as Nick's, Vincent's, Ralph's, George's, Electric Haze, Guertin's. (I'm not kidding, I want to make this happen. A tour of art you can see in a bar in town. A little guide book and a description of the art. More on this as we move forward)

There was an old school bar shuffle board in the second room and it was cool, but I do recall a bar owner looking down on things like that. It takes up room and doesn't make money for the bar. Not a good thing, in the opinion of this one bar owner. On the other hand, it was pretty cool.

Before I go on. I like the bar. It was clean and presentable and fun. And now...

Here is my problem with it. The idea that the bar has a theme. That it is a political bar. I don't like the idea that the bar can force a theme on any establishment. How can Mr. Glodis say that it will be a political joint. Are people forced to talk about Trump or Warren or McGovern?

Will they pass out conversation starters? Will you be cut off for talking about movies or sports or knitting techniques?

It brings to mind when I take my eight year son out for dinner and he looks at me seriously and states, "Now we will have a talk Daddy. We will talk about our favorite characters from the Harry Potter books." Or we will talk about what is the best Star Wars movie. Or it is decreed to be only what the best part of the Dr. Strange movie was.

And for my son, I will jump into that conversation with crazed enthusiasm. But going to a bar, where I paid more than six bucks for my gin and tonic, I don't know if I will be so enticed. "And now, Daddy, we will talk about the issues of the second amendment in regards to immigration." I guess we could have that talk, but I don't know if I would like it as much as saying that Lucius Mallfoy is my favorite Harry Potter bad guy.

Give a bar credit. Let it be what it wants. It might be called the Ballot Box. But the only politics of it is that it is a Meat Market, or a Gay Bar, a Sport Bar, or a high end joint to have a good drink in a clean glass. None of those are bad, of course. But all of those are not pushed upon the bar by the owners. Let the customers determine what it is. Let the customers tell you what kind of a bar they are drinking in.

Until Next Time,

Dante of Worcester

2020 Update: *This is closed. I only went the one time. There is a sign saying what it will be next time, but at the moment, it is still just an empty space.*

Letter Two - Gin and Tonics at Yummy Steakhouse

Dear Worcester,

Since the last time, I went to two more bars and had gin and tonics. Well, they are both restaurants with bars. There is a big distinction. It's the big question of this walking around and settling in for a drink and then walking to the next place. The question, are you in a bar with food, are you at a restaurant where you can get a drink? It's where you place the emphasis. Like how you say Aunt. Do you say it like Ant or Ahnt. I say it like Ant, which must mean I prefer to go into a bar with food. If the bar doesn't have food, or if the kitchen has been accidentally phased into another realm of existence and then only thing available is liquor, I am fine with that state of affairs.

I went to two last Wednesday. I hit Yummy Steak House and Leo's. Both of them are definitely Restaurants with bars attached to them. For this letter, I think I will only talk about Yummy. I have enough to say about Leo's and I don't want to overwhelm you with my comments, because you know me, how I do go on and on. There is no stopping me.

Actually, that is not completely true. I have one drink on this expedition of bars and then I am done. I don't do food, I just have one gin and tonic and move along. I always write like I walk from bar to bar. From place to place. Like some western Palladin, Have Drink Card Will Travel. But the truth is, there is no way to go from place to place in Worcester without a car. It kind of takes a little of the mystique out of a bar excursion.

Yummy Steak House is a Sushi Bar, Hibachi joint, and Asian restaurant. On its off hours, it also fights crime. 1121 Grafton Street is where it is. Another Asian restaurant was there before this. The bones of it is what you would expect. A large area for hibachi tables, a room with a colorful bar, tables for diners and an area for the sushi to be made. There was keno and sports on the flat screen. There were bright neon colors for accent. Nothing out of place. Well, maybe I was out of place.

Because I wasn't eating. There were folks at the bar, but all ot them were having drinks and appetizers, as you should. The bartender gave me a menu. The manager asked if I needed some little snack to help soak up all that good booze sloshing in my belly. He actually didn't say it like that, he was very polite. The drink was alright, good enough, for 7.50. If you are at a restaurant with a license to sling booze, you are truly odd man out if you just want a drink. I mean, how many people come to this place you have to drive to and is known for their hibachi and not their cocktails and just get a mixed drink? Not a hell of a lot. They didn't throw me out, naturally, I was there and it was fine.

I hear good things about the food. That it is a really good hibachi joint and the sushi is good as well. But that is all hearsay. But that's not what I want to talk to you about. It's about the name. Yummy.

The place is called Yummy. I can't help myself. I want to mock it. I want to make fun of it. I want to say that that is the dumbest name for a restaurant ever. That is courting so many dismissive comments. It's an accident waiting to happen.

That's what I want to do, and I guess I did. But I want to couch it. One is a friend heard I went there and said its cultural. That some Asian places name themselves that way. My friend said the best sushi he ever had was a place in California called Happy Sushi.

The next thing is that I have a bartender friend who says yummy. He will make a complicated cocktail and taste it and say, "That's yummy." That's right, the only person I know who says yummy on a regular basis is referring to coladas and mojito variations.

Maybe we should say it more. Maybe we would be a happier people if grown men and women could go to a place and call it yummy. Would there less wars? Would racial antagonism dissipate and recede like a summer rain? Would be worthy of being yummy in a yummy world?

I heard the food is yummy. The well gin and tonic was basic and just passable, but that's just a well highball. We are not judging it by its sushi or its hibachi flaming onion. We are judging it on its side effort. It's a nice place to sit and watch the Keno numbers. Maybe the food is yummy.

One would hope.

Until Next Time

Dante

Letter Three - Bars and Poetry

Dear Worcester,

Every now and then, heading for home, I will stop by Breen's Cafe to have a beer and watch a little of the Bruins game. I only want to stop there if the Bruins are playing, don't ask me why. For whatever reason, if I get the chance, that's where I want to watch hockey.

Last week, the Bruins were playing and I was driving by, so I stopped and got a beer (this is not one of those letters where I write about a new bar to try a gin and tonic in. This is a letter about being at a bar in Worcester and what I and others find in those moments. I figure I will share these with you, if you don't mind.) The Bruins were doing just fine and the beer was cold.

People were talking and having a nice time.

And then I had to use the men's room.

It's a bar. There is beer. This is an act that occurs often in such an establishment. I went into the stall and noticed a linen tea towel framed and hung above the toilet. There was a poem on the towel, an old yellowing thing. Around the words were the pearly gates, bottles of spirits, a glass of wine. The things you expect in a bar. Well, maybe not the pearly gates. But that is in the poem.

Let me give you the words to the poem that greeted me in the bathroom stall in Breen's.

He deserves a hero's medal for the many lives he's saved, And upon the Roll of Honour his name should be engraved. He deserves a lot of credit for the way he stands the strain. For the yarns he has to swallow would drive most of us insane.

He must pay the highest licence, he must pay the highest rent. He must battle with his bank and pay their ten percent. And when it comes to paying bills, he's always on the spot. He pays for what he sells, whether you pay him or not.

And when you walk into his Bar, he'll greet you with a smile. Be you a workman dressed in overalls or a banker dressed in style. If you're Irish English Scotch or Welsh, it doesn't matter what. He'll treat you like a gentleman, unless you prove you're not. Yet the clergy in the pulpit and the preacher in the hall. Will assure him that the Churches are against him one and all. But when the Churches plan to hold a ballot or bazaar. They start by selling tickets to the man behind the bar.

When he retires a job well done, to await six feet of soil, Discards his coat and apron, no more on earth to toil. As Saint Peter sees him coming, he will leave those gates ajar. For he knows he had his Hell on Earth, THE MAN BEHIND THE BAR

Now let me say that I didn't read the poem there. I just realized what it was and took a picture of it on my phone. I then did a search and found it on the internet. Cut and paste and here it is. I didn't do much heavy lifting. I learned that this poem has been around for a long time. In some places, the poet is Hasty Peter. Hasty writing from Hasty Peter. But for the most part it is an anonymous poem to be read in a bar for a bar audience.

Which brings up the question, was I expected to read it right there in the toilet stall? Was I going to give my much respected private time to the reading of bar poetry? In the past, were there lines for the john as people finished reading the fine literature waiting for them there?

Before cell phone cameras and internet searches, how did anyone read poetry in public? Did people stand in front of framed tea towels in bars across the county and quietly and conscientiously study the words of the beer soaked bards? Was there slurred discussion of metaphor and hyperbole? Well, there is always metaphor and hyperbole in every bar conversation.

Have we lost one of the great joys of bar going? The reading of accidental literature? I have already said that there needs to be an art walk of bars. Do we need a poetry walk through bars as well? I don't know if that's necessary, there is so much poetry in bars to begin with.

Now don't get me wrong. I love that Breen's has this piece of doggerel in the bathroom. It feels like what an Irish sports bar should do. It is honest and fun. I know of a few bars that put up the sports page behind plexiglass above bathroom urinals. Getting a tea towel poem is just so much better than the Red Sox box scores.

The poem ain't much. And it is a little exaggerated about the plight of the man behind the bar, and the rhyme scheme is a little haggard. But like I said, a bar should always have poetry in it, even the stilted kind.

Till Next Time

Dante of Worcester

Letter Four - Gin and Tonics at Leo's

Dear Worcester,

Leo's is a neon sign on Shrewsbury Street. It's a fancy curlicue sign with red letters that states "Leo's." It makes you think of old times on the shore with the family back when men wore hats. That's all it ever was for me in the near two decades I have lived in and around Worcester. An art installation more than a restaurant.

The restaurant proper is a few hundred paces back away from the street. I never felt the need to go there. I never heard of anyone recommending it. The only thing I might have been told is that it used to be a great old school Italian place, but now the kids are running it and it's not what it used to be. You hear that thing all the time. "The kids don't have the heart the old man had for the joint." That has been said as long as there have been family businesses. It doesn't mean that it is true.

I have had no desire to try it out for the gin and tonic tour. Maybe because every time I mentioned it, people would pshaw it and say it ain't worth it. So I skipped it when I hit 144 places for gin and tonics and the world did not break asunder. I came back to do the new bars and restaurants last year and Leo's didn't even cross my mind. Now, here I am on the third go round of bars in Worcester and I figured that I might hit the places I overlooked or ignored. While sitting in a doctor's waiting room, I made a list of joints to hit and get a gin and tonic. For some reason, I caught myself writing down Leo's. And so that is how it happened.

At 6:45 on a Wednesday (during restaurant week) I parked the car and walked down what felt like a back alley to the front of Leo's. I wasn't sure. It felt like a lobby to a forgotten hotel. I found the door and on my right was the mostly empty dining room. I was greeted with a mass produced sign that said, "Seat yourself."

Okay, call me a snob. But if I want to seat myself, I will get my dinner at a food truck and find a nice bench to rest upon. If I am going to a restaurant that is not known to be cheap, I want someone to greet me at the door with pleasant efficiency. I want them to look at the table chart and find me the best and proper table. I want a smile and a, "This way please." Is that so much to ask?

Apparently so. No one even acknowledged my confused presence.

I had to navigate the strange old setting myself. I looked down a short hallway and thought it was a good bet there might be a bar there. The pictures on the wall were family portraits, the owner and his wife I guess. It was more like going through a hallway in a friend's family house, looking for the bathroom. It took some time for me to find the bar area, or at least a place to have a drink.

I did find the bar and had an eight dollar gin and tonic. Do I have to even state that it was okay at best? The bartenders seemed preoccupied. There were three couples there at the bar, all eating and drinking. None of the food looked appetizing. They were just pasta with red sauce glopped on it like it was an Italian Restaurant themed horror movie: On Top of Satan's Spaghetti, all covered in gore!!!

Outside of one of the bartenders, I was the youngest one there by about two decades. And I'm in my late forties. No one was excited to be there. It was the day to go out eating and so they were. I tried to think of something to write about but was stymied. The place is a tired joint filled with tired people.

To make my point, the bathroom has an ad on the wall for Charlton Manor Rest Home/ Assisted Living. I'm not knocking it, they know the right place to advertise. The copy reads in part "We are a small elegant home with many special features, you will feel like you are visiting a Bed and Breakfast or an Old Inn." Which is different from the feel at Leo's - the Neon Sign that Walks Like a Dining Location.

On the wall of the bar area was a large painting that no doubt was purchased at Home Goods. It had a young stylish woman in a black dress at a bar. The bar was classic wood and was inviting. The view was from behind. Her head was turned so you spied her in profile. She held a martini glass aloft. She seemed poised and pleased. I thought to myself, "Why can't I go there?"

Well that was snarkier than I thought it would be.

Until next time,

Dante of Worcester

Letter Five - Gin and Tonics at the Usual

Dear Worcester

Last Sunday, I celebrated a little time off with a trip to Shrewsbury Street. I have a few new places on that ever mutable street to try. I am not going into the British Beer Company for a gin and tonic because it's a chain and the world is too big and my liver is too small for me to include chain joints on the tour of places to drink. Case in point, I went into the Usual for a highball cocktail. It is located at 166 Shrewsbury Street. Before the Usual, this was the spot for the Fix. Before that it was Mezcal Cafe. Before that it was Goodfellas. And before that it was a ground level entrance to the Underworld (little known fact).

The Usual is a high end, gourmet sandwich place. It's fine dining between two hunks of bread. Ah the humble Sandwich. According to a reliable source, namely Jack Palance in an episode of Ripley's Believe it or Not, the Sandwich was created in order to continue gambling. It was a convenience to throwing your money away, like the Instant Scratch Ticket.

The story that Jack Palance said in his ominous voice was that the Earl of Sandwich loved gambling with cards. Loved it. He was just lousy at it. One night he was losing hard and someone asked to stop playing so they could repair to the dining room and have supper. But Earl was having none of it. He was feeling a lucky streak coming on and he didn't want to stop, not when the luck was returning. It wasn't, of course. Earl was an easy mark. He said, "Nuts, I ain't leaving with this hand burning my fingers. No way. Just cut up some roast and put it in between two hunks of bread and bring it to me here."

And that, my friends, is how genius works.

And like most stories that stick with you for decades, it has nothing to do with what I am writing about. I just wanted to prove that I know the real skinny about the Sandwich. And now, so do you. Believe it, or not.

The Usual. I walked in at 1:45 on this Sunday afternoon. Four or five of the tables were occupied. At the bar were three groups of people drinking and eating. The bar is in the same place as it was in the last two restaurants that squatted at this address. There was still a tiered dining space, with the top section empty except for an employee texting on her phone.

It is a clean, simple design. Perhaps we can say boring, but we don't have to go there. Let's call it minimal and leave it at that. Two guys were on my left drinking Heinekens talking passionately about people and business. On my right were two other guys hardly speaking to each other. They drank their waters and waited for their sandwiches, occasionally looking up from their phones to tell about a show they streamed or a video that is pretty funny. They might have come from a run or a work out. Or they might have just stumbled out of bed from a long heroic night of Saturday evening carousing. It was impossible to figure out which was true.

The bartender was bubbly, full of smiles and interest. I got my 8 dollar and forty cent gin and tonic and drank it like it was any gin and tonic. That's the nice thing about a cocktail. It doesn't care how much money it is sold for. It is a happy worker and could care less if it goes for three bucks or nine. It supplies the taste and the bubble and the hint of lime no matter what the sticker price states. A gin and tonic is a proud thing and doesn't care about worth.

The Usual was a lazy, sleepy Sunday bar. The food looked fine. Everything was sedate. But it is Sunday after a long Saturday, does anyone want loud laughter and music? I actually was not sure if there was any music playing there. For the most part it was silent, like a liquor license monastery. On rare moments with the wind blowing, I could swear I was hearing eighties pop lightly going on somewhere else in the room. This place was made to nurse hangovers.

I left after about twenty minutes feeling that the place was alright, a nice upclass joint for common man food. But I was vaguely dissatisfied. Was this what a Sunday afternoon bar was? Sedate to the edge of coma?

I was walking to my car, parked further down on Shrewsbury Street, and on one of those whims that I wished I trusted more, I walked past my car and looked for another place on the Street that possibly could be more lively. Or maybe I would find every place dead.

I heard voices and aimed for it. I went into the Wormtown Brewery Tap Room. The place was pretty full. About 40 or 50 folk were in there drinking the beer, showing off their flannel shirts and knit caps. If Shrewsbury Street was charted by antiquarian cartographers for a navigational map to sail successfully through this restaurant row, they would have labeled Wormtown Brewery with the admonition, "Here there be hipsters."

People were in groups laughing and telling tales and explaining why this beer is superior to other beers and giving long winded evidence for their opinions. I got their Belgian White and it was good, perhaps too hoppy for a white in my tasting, but I was still charmed by the people and the talk and the cheer found on a rainy Sunday.

There was a kid, about nine or ten, with his family. The kid was not drinking (officer) but was focusing on his earbuds and his music. He didn't seem put out, he was happy enough being ignored by the grownups. On seeing him, it put me in mind to all the times I have seen kids in bars. I was lost in thought, leaning against a small tract of wall.

I finished my beer and finally got back to my car. So I saw two types of Sunday afternoons. Silent, sedate, quiet and empty. A place to regroup from a long weekend. Decent food in a decent place. And then there was the place to have the new beer and talk loudly to be heard. A reminder that Sunday afternoon does not mean that the fun and the socialization has to be over.

Neither of them are bad. I can see myself picking either of them on different days, with different moods. It depends on the place my head is at.

That's it for now, till next time.

Dante

2020 Update: *Let me see if I get this right. This place was swept up in a federal sting. The owner was arrested and this other properties were closed down. It opened up at Chameleon and that lasted for a hot second. It is now the Meze Estiatoria.*

Letter Six - Bars and Children

Dear Worcester,

In the last letter I wrote about my time at the Wormtown Brewery (a fine place if I neglected to state that before) and spied a kid around nine or ten with his family or extended family. He was safe in his smart phone and earbuds and had an impenetrable shield that protected him from the packs of knit capped hipsters appreciating the IPA like it was fine wine gone to vinegar.But it made me think about kids in drinking joints.

Every family has its own tradition of how to introduce their progeny into the ever present world of drinking. Wine at Sunday Dinner. Manischewitz during Passover. A can of Schlitz at their first Packers game for Cheese Heads across the globe.

My friend Bob always tried to ply beer or wine on my son, even when he was an infant. It was a joke. Especially because my response to these vaudevillian attempts was to state. "Not until he's five."

This was because my first beer was when I was five. I remember it clearly. A bunch of the fathers in our neighborhood were drinking Pabst in our driveway and we boys were pestering. One of the boys asked his dad for a sip and he got it. Score! So the next boy asked his dad for a sip and he got it. And I asked for a sip next and got it. Boy did I get it. Straight from the can. The aluminum did nothing but improve the taste. Then one of us, maybe Paul Anderson, asked if he could have another sip and his father responded, "No, get your own."

Get your own. The ultimate DIY statement of independence. It's the Beatles realizing that they don't have to settle for Pete Best Backbeats. It was Sam Houston comprehending that this state can be their state. It was Allen Ginsberg stating that the slithery flow of words and imagery that his soul composed must be poetry. It's Jonny Rotten concluding that music was whatever anger fit into three cords and dissonance. It was someone saying, "Hey you midwestern kid, wouldn't more of that yellow bubbly elixir be the best way to end the day?" Get your own. Do it yourself.

Paul looked at us boys and said, "We have beer in our house. We can get our own there." So we three boys trooped over to his house and got Schlitz and dutifully sipped at those damned cans of endless cans of unpleasantness while sitting on the back stoop. But we were now men and there was no place for complaint. We drank at our cans like dogma. When the adults realized that the evening was too peaceful, they searched for us. They found us and ducked in corners to laugh at what they saw. Only when they laughter was done did they come and seriously remove us from our beers.

That was how I came up with the "Only when he's five" line. When my son turned five, I was petrified that Bob would keep me to it. Only last week, when my son was eight, did Bob bring it up. We were all at a Nick's for a PFLAG benefit where he said, "You told me that he could have beer at five, we are well past that." My wife organized the benefit up but couldn't attend so me and the kid were there. My lame response to Bob was, "You didn't ask him when he was five so you missed your chance."

Bob rolled his eyes at that, so I turned to the boy and asked, "Bob wants to get you a beer, you want it."

My son looked at me oddly and said. "I have chocolate milk." And that was it. I felt more relief than I can say. Yes, I would not have given the beer if he did ask for it, but it was pleasant to not come across the consequence.

Off and on for three years, my son has been going into Nick's. I run a bi weekly event there and sometimes I have to bring him. The bartender Sean, one of my closest friends, always greets him warmly and has him make a mixed fruit juice concoction to drink through the event. My son adores Sean.

A few weeks ago my kid stated that for a job, he would like to help Sean out behind the bar. He would get him the beers. Grab him the ice. Do whatever Sean needed to be a good bartender.

I don't know, but I am not sure that a lot of high school guidance counselors recommend "bar back" as a career goal.

About a year and a half ago, he reported to us that one of his schoolmates said he wanted to be a bartender when he grew up, because a bartender gets all the ladies. We asked him what "gets all the ladies" meant, and he only stared at us. I told Sean and he informed me that that estimation of a bartender's life is not exactly accurate. And wait a minute? Why is a second grader interested in the ladies in the first place?

There is nothing wrong with taking a child to a place that has liquor. It is unavoidable. Last year, I went into the Oaken Barrel for a gin and tonic and there were three women at the bar drinking and swearing. Swearing like you will only see in Worcester and Quentin Tarrantino films. One of the colorful talkers had her seven year old son with her. He wasn't on a stool, drinking and cussin. No he was running around the tables. Some of the tables had people eating there, but that didn't matter. It was a dull uninteresting place for this kid and he was making his own fun.

It's like those uncomfortable kid's birthday parties that we parents stand around, wishing to be anywhere else. You don't know the people, you don't know what to say, all you do is watch your kid and all these other running noses and skinned knees scream bloody murder and call it a fine time. Many of them are at bowling alleys. Here in New England we wave candlepin bowling, the perfect type of bowling for kids. They can hold onto the ball. They can also easily bash them over their friend's heads. But hey, birthday parties are so much fun.

There is something weird to me when I see one of these parents get a beer from the bowling alley bar and continue watching the kids run around like they are radioactive particles racing up to nuclear fission. I know that there is nothing wrong with having a beer in front of kids, but this is the kid's world and an adult beverage seems like a breaking of a trust. I want one of the kids to go up to the grown up drinking the bottle of Bud and say, "Excuse me, do you mind? We children don't traipse down to your over 21 fetes at the Ship Room at the Hotel Vernon and demand chocolate milk shakes and watch you get sloppy as you drunkenly sing karaoke, then why are you drinking your beverage at our bowling party?" Yes. These are the things I think about at these parties. I am that bored.

There are times when kids have to go into bars.

Like when they are tasked to retrieve their drunken father. I feel like I am in the first chapter of a Horatio Alger novel (before it all turns perfect) and that this doesn't happen, but come on, we know it does.

I got a buddy in town who gets angry when we go by certain streets. That was the street, he informs me, where his Dad's bar was. His Dad didn't own it, he just contributed to it by drinking himself senseless. He didn't drink himself to death there, only because there were other bars, not to mention the package stores. It was my friend's and his brother's job to find him and roust him home.

The bar is gone, but the anger still percolates, still bubbles, like a cut reopening and becoming infected once more. I never pressed details. I didn't ask him how often he had to go into the dark bar. How scared he was? Was it such a typical chore that the drunks on the stool would greet him by name? I am always curious about those things, but decided it is best not to ask. He still gets angry just being near the street. Like the bar is a ghost haunting him, wailing and moaning in the voice of old Patsy Cline 45s.

The only thing close to funny about this story is my friend tends bar at a few joints in the city. He sometimes pours beers to old timers, some of whom sat next to his father in the long ago bar. There is not enough liquor in all the bars of Worcester to mask the acrid taste of sad irony in those moments.

For me, I didn't have to find my father in bars. Though I am sure he knew quite a few of them. He had a homemade bar in the basement in our house in Naperville Illinois. We kids would use it in our make believe play as the cockpit for the Millennium Falcon.

When my father came home for the day from his high clearance government job (he did something with nuclear weapons, we are not sure exactly what) he would greet me by saying my name and then raising two fingers. That was my prompt to go downstairs and get two cans of beer from the basement fridge. He would be seated at the kitchen table, removing his tie by the time I placed them in front of him. That still is the only bartending job I ever had.

By the time I turned nine, my father had been dead for six months. Heart attack. I was becoming a troubled kid. School was not going well for me. My mother thought that what I needed was a male influence.

I don't know where she found this guy, but she got this psychology grad student to hang out with me once a week and be my buddy. I must have been a tough nut to crack because after only a few months he ran out of fun things to do with me.

So, he took me to his bar.

It was in downtown Naperville and it had the green glass and low back stools of an Irish Bar you ordered from a kit. Ostensibly, we went there to play pool and ping pong. But really, he just felt more at ease dealing with this weird kid when he could sit at his bar and be in his safe environment.

We sat at the stools and he had me order root beer for both of us. The mugs were very foamy. By the third time we were there the bartender greeted me by name.

I am sure we played pool much longer than we were sitting at the bar, but that's the part I recall with any clarity. It was the part that stuck with me.

He stopped hanging out with me soon after. I think I might have told my mother I was not interested in spending time with him, though I am not sure. It was a hell of a long time ago.

There are some of us who love going to bars. Adore the sensation of the stool. The grasp of the cold beer mug, the soul cool of the dark wood interior. If you are lucky to find that place you want to share it. You take your loved ones there. You introduce your girlfriend, your boyfriend, to the regulars with regal formality. Why wouldn't you want your kid to see the place? To appreciate that wonderful world that is your bar, the bar?

So you have to watch the kid, do you have to abandon your bar life? Well, that is a fine question. A real question. It depends on what you are looking for. It depends on what you think your child needs to learn.

And please do not disregard that last statement. There are lessons for little ones to learn at any bar. That drunk adults are silly. That bartenders have the coolest jobs and that will be a fine thing to be when and if you grow up. That "get your own" is a worthy concept, but that is different from help yourself (bar owners tend to frown at that). Remember that "get your own" is the first step on the road to "be on your own." That drinking root beer at the bar might be the basement make believe version of feeling like a man. That despite the countless times you are sent into the bar to bring your father home, you might never find him. That he is no where to be found. No matter how many doors you open, or how many pint glasses you lift to see what hides underneath, nestled with the coasters, forgotten in the well.

Till Next Time

David

Letter 7 - Gin and Tonics at the Pint

Dear Worcester

It is amazing what happens to my mind after going to 160 different bars in Worcester, everything begins to seem the same. Actually, it is not that it seems the same, it actually is. The same. I am going to the same bars again. Now more than ever.

I started this project over three years ago and for a long stretch of that, most of the bars were places I had never been before. The buildings were new, the people I sat next to were new. Everything about the process had a aire of exploration. But we are now past that sense of newness. Now I am going back to the same places because they are now new bars, new restaurants.

The old bar went out of business, or the owner retired, or the place decided that it desired a new skin, a new name and now it was something wholly unique.

In this version of the tour, I have been to five bars and three of them are places I was at before. I like going into joints I never been to before. I like that sense of fear. That apprehension. That surprise that the place is good looking or feels bigger inside than it does from the street. I like that self imposed vertigo of being the new guy in town.

But what I feel now is deja vu. "Oh, that hasn't changed from when it was the other bar." "Look at that, they just cleaned the bar and called it new." "Look at that, they didn't clean the bar and now it has a new name." There are differences of course. The walls are now orange. The bartenders now wear ties. Oh, how I miss going to a part of town I never have been and go into a building I have never entered before.

All of this was on mind when I was at The Pint, 58 Shrewsbury Street. This used to be Scorz, which I thought was one of the lousiest bars I have been to for a gin and tonic. The place had a weird lay out and it just made me sad. The people who worked there that night seemed to be unhappy to be there. I was not surprised to hear it went out of business. I mean if the folks pouring your beer don't want to be there, why do you?

The Pint was filling up and people were having fun, talking loud. At nine, the door man took his place, expecting the flood to appear. It is a bar. A pretty decent one. The gin and tonic was seven fifty and was alright. That's another piece of deja vu. All the well originated gin and tonics taste like the ones I had before. I took a sip, and then asked the drink, "Haven't we met before? Perhaps on a Mediterranean cruise?

What makes the Pint unique is the white elephant jumble sale that are the walls. Every wall has a lot of art or posters or tchakes. To call it eclectic gives the art presentation more premeditation than it probably deserves. This is not me complaining. If an art museum suddenly became a live, sentient being, this would be it's subconscious. This is an art collection's fever dream. I took pictures of one small wall and the art there. In the space of three feet we have: a print of children and a dog hiding in a nook of a tree, an ugly framed folk art portrait of a girl who looks like she is fifty years old and balding, a pastel of hands, a photo of a goldfish blowing bubbles out of a wine glass filled with water, all next to what I think is a walking stick mounted to the wall. Other walls have a portrait of Boba Fett and other pop culture wall hangings.

It definitely has a personality. Is it the personality of a bar you want to drink in? That's up to you. It wasn't my thing, but I watched people ambling in, the bar getting busy. Maybe the decor means nothing. Maybe the sense of sameness and deja vu is just a passing phase. Maybe I should just shut up and order another drink. It doesn't matter what wall art or architectural space you are wrapped in, just drink up and enjoy.

Until Next Time

Dante

Letter 8 - Bars and Dating

Dear Worcester,

I was talking to a friend who still talks about his ex. His ex who he met at his bar. He has a bar he likes. He caught the eye of a woman who also called the bar her own. They had something in common. They both liked the same bar. There are long lived marriages based on less than that.

Now he doesn't talk to the ex. He talks about her. To me. To other guys at the bar. But not to her.

They were a couple in the bar for over a year. They were a pair on display, a happy couple that old drunks watched with jealousy and watery eyes. They proved that bars and couples are a perfect combination. They were pleasant to talk to together or separate.

But sometimes a relationship based on feeling at home in the same piece of real estate doesn't have enough sustenance to survive. They broke up. Then, quietly, they got back together. They went on holiday together. They told us funny stories of their vacation. They were happy and it looked just like before, the happy couple we knew.

In a month, they were broken up again.

Now here we are. A couple that is no more. We see both them. She is with a new partner. He is focusing on his job and school, but still comes here. It is his bar after all. There is something important about that act of claiming: that "This Bar Is Mine." It is an ancient and holy rite, to pick the bar of your soul. I am sure she feels the same way. Sucks that both of them chose the same place.

The bartender and I both say, that's the problem. Don't date from your bar. Nothing good can come from that.

I saw my friend today and we stood drinking Guinness and talking about the situation. I should capitalize it and call it the Situation. Like an annoying camera hog from the Jersey Shore. It won't stop mugging for attention.

My friend doesn't waste much time talking about other things, the conversation gets to the ex. "So here's an example. This explains what I'm talking about. The other day I get here after work and I want to have a few drinks. I want to just drink by myself. The commute to work is killing me, but work is good. I got a raise, but they expect me to work harder for that and you know, I'm trying to finish up grad school. I'm exhausted and all I want is to have a few drinks and not talk to anyone."

Let me pause to say, that to me, that is one of the great mysteries about going to a bar. It allows you a spectrum of social possibilities. You can be greeted like Norm in Cheers or you can say hello and get back to your crossword or you can sit moping in front of your mug and no one will bother you. That's one of the first things you learn as a bar goer, how to read the shoulders of a guy at the bar. You have to read it right. If they are hunched forward, leave that man alone. He is only here to visit his dear friend, the one in the glass, and share a whispered word. That's the thing about bars. Course, a lot of people get it wrong. Yes, going to a bar is like learning a new language. And its slurred and full of marbles.

My friend goes on, "I am just drinking. Even the bartender knew to nod at me and let me be. Then the girl came in. With her new guy. I don't know the guy. I'm sure I don't like him, but don't pin me on it. But the thing is they are at the end of the bar and I'm right there by the door, I'm not noticing them. I got to say that again. I am not bothering them. I am just by myself drinking. That's all. I'm not thinking about her. She says hi to me and I don't say nothing. She's in the bar with her new guy, but I got drinking to do, I got a day to erase. Important things. And she comes over to me. Now I wasn't looking at her, not even a sideways glance. But she comes over to me all serious and says I won't say hi if you don't want me to and I said, and this is all I said, I said let's do that. I just want status quo here. I just want to drink.

"Dave, isn't that what I was implying just from drinking at my bar, sitting by myself, talking to no one? Isn't that what I was saying? I mean the act of not looking at anyone and drinking, that's talking truth to power, right? That's saying a lot, or it should. Someone should see that and know that. Anyway, she goes back to her spot at the bar and I'm focusing on my crossword and my beer. Then she comes up again and says that they are going to be playing a dice game and I can come down and play with them.

"That's what she said. That I can come down and play a dice game with them. Just twenty minutes before, she says we should avoid and ignore each other and now she wants to play a dice game with me. I give her a look, and say, I thought you didn't want to acknowledge me. And if we don't want to notice each other, why are you asking me to play a dice game? She shut her face and nodded with a grimace. And she goes back to her guy and I go back to my beer but I can't really go back to my beer because now I'm pondering what the hell that was all about?

"What the hell? What did I do wrong there? What is stopping me from being at a bar, a bar I like, and just be myself? Why do I have to think about this? I don't want to think about this. I am happy never even thinking about her. I just want to drink at my bar by myself. Why is that such a difficult proposition?"

He and I speak of this for a while. I wonder when we will be done with this conversation. I wonder when the bar will return to stasis. When the status quo is people talking to each other, ignoring each, getting drunk with each other, lost in thought and never to return? When will that state show up?

The bartender and I both say, that's the problem. Don't date from your bar. Nothing good can come of it.

Until next time,

David

Letter Nine - Gin and Tonics at Bull Mansion

Dear Worcester,

"So you are a reviewer," the bar back said to me with a conspiratorial grin pleasantly widening on his face.

Reviewer, I don't think that's the proper name for me. I just go to a bar I have never been to and sit myself down and order a gin and tonic. I don't eat at the places. I don't stay an evening. I don't enrobe myself in the atmosphere. I am here and gone. A dilettante. An itinerant drinker.

Never to put roots down and call this stool my own.

And then I write it down like an ancient mariner with a martini olive around my neck instead of a dead waterfowl.

"No," I said to the bar back, "just a guy having a drink."

"You have to try the food." This is what you say to a reviewer whose opinion means something. Not to me. I am a blogger (a terrible person with a terrible monicker), I am a writer of letters that might as well be written to myself.

"Oh I will. But I'm just having a drink." The bar back smiled larger and stared at me, like he knew a secret, a really cool secret.

Hell with it. I drank my cocktail quickly and walked out. I was caught. And I didn't realize that one of the best parts about doing this tour of every bar in Worcester is that I can do this without anyone knowing what I am doing. That I am just what I appear to be, only another guy at a bar wanting to have a drink. Wanting to get lost in a glass.

The place I left quickly, was a new bistro on Pearl Street called Bull Mansion. It is actually an old mansion. Let me just say that it was lovely. The bar is small, but people are not there to drink. People were going upstairs to a Cocker Rocks show, I guess someone who played with Joe Cocker has a tribute show. Others were eating outside on the patio.

It was seven o'clock and people were dressed up and scented and ready to enjoy the confluence of pleasant weather and a Saturday evening. What a joy to have both things happen at the same time. Let's sit in a beautiful environment and eat food, which a bar back assured was very good.

There was art on the walls, but my hasty retreat impeded my ability to tell you about it. Reviewer he called me. Would a reviewer have busted out before getting all the information on the joint? I don't think so.

The stools at the marble bar are simple and they struck as me as perfect. No back on them, only a circle of wood attached to some metal. The bartenders were busy filling up the table order. I waited five minutes for her to acknowledge me. I must have had my"I am a very important person and I hate being ignored at a half full bar" face because she apologized to me about the wait. I tried to be cool with it. But I am not adept at nonchalance.

I got a Bombay Sapphire gin and tonic in a large water glass (a nice water glass, but I am just trying to be accurate here). She asked if I want a lime, of course I do. This was how a drink should be. A good amount of both gin and tonic. I enjoyed the drink, but that was until I had to swig that bad boy down and get out of there because of the grinning bar back. The drink was eight dollars.

There is a relaxed elegance to the place. People dress up a little bit. They are happy to be out. To be with friends. The bar is not a place to hang out and read the paper. This is the launch area before the table is ready. People came and got their martini glass drinks and talked loud.

If I have one complaint about Bull Mansion is the smell of it. Let me explain. The other day I went into the Ghanaian restaurant in town, Anokye Krom, to have a Guinness and I was greeted not only with friendly people and a cold beer but the wonderful aromas of stews and meats and spices. The place smelled like a good restaurant. It invited you to sit and drink and wait excitedly for the food to come.

At Bull Mansion, I was not enticed with the aroma of the food. I actually got no whiff of a chop or anything else. That was because all I smelled was everyone's perfume and cologne. Every time someone walked by, I was assaulted with another smell from laboratories. You got Chanel and Old Spice and I'm sure one of the guys was doused in Canoe (for the seventies throwback feel). It was a lot of impressing everyone with the odor you bathe your body in. And hey? What's that smell of Patchouli doing there?

I could not taste the botanical notes in my gin and tonic with all these invading scents breaching.

But that was a minor complaint. It is a complaint about going out on a Saturday night. Might as well complain about women wearing ridiculously precarious high heels for all the good it will do.

I think I would have given this a short but enthusiastic little write up if it wasn't for Maitre D Mal (Mal is short for a Malcom, or Malcontent. I can never remember which one it is) He spied me as he set up a table. He smiled and I gave him a conspiratorial nod. He knew about this blog.

It was when I had the drink to my lips and was thinking of what I would say of it, what makes this gin and tonic different from any other, when Maitre D Mal came over draping his arm around me. "Are you having a gin and tonic? Are you doing your thing?"

"I'm having a drink," I said haughtily. "Just minding my business."

Mal didn't get my leave me alone look, or rather, he didn't give a shit. I'm writing about the place he's working. How nice. He asked about the recent entries to the blog. I answered quickly. He hugged me and went off. And that's when the bar back, who had been listening asked that question that you all recall so clearly from the top of this letter, "So you are a reviewer?"

What am I anyway, I asked, as I quickly retreated. How was it that the Bull Mansion created such a moment of existential crisis inside me? Am I critic, a blogger, a reviewer, a nuisance, a walrus, a carpenter? So many choices.

The truth is I am a writer. I am a drinker. I am guy who is putting the two together and attempting to live to tell the tale.

Let us hope that next time I will not be seen. I will just be the extra in somebody else's drama. I am just a witness. The kind that tips and leaves.

Until next time

Dante.

Letter 10 - Gin and Tonics at the Bootleggers Prohibition Pub

Dear Worcester

What is there to say about a dull restaurant bar closing its doors and rebranding themselves as something that is different but still dull? What am I to say about this? How shall I be a pleasant host and guide if this is my thesis and the constant theme I will be whistling?

How shall I do this? With a smile on my face and a bounce to my step.

It's moments like this that make me happy to be a crass, cynical writer. It gets to be a drag writing pleasantly about pleasant places. Bring on the banal, I got my mean spirited adjectives sharpened and holstered at the end of each sentence.

Storytime: Once there was a health food store on Park Avenue and Chandler Street and it was good. Their wheat germ was the finest of the realm. And lo, they decided that they should have a restaurant in the same location and that was good. And it became Evo, which (I think) was in reference to it being the next level of Evolution of cuisine. Those health food folk are nothing if not humble.

Evo had a nice run of several years. The bar in the back was small and inconsequential and despite what others said, I thought the food was pretty mediocre, if not bad. The last time we had food there, it was downright inedible. That is always a good sign that a joint is going to go out of business.

But not in this fairy tale, brother. In this one, the wounded beast retreated into the cocoon that we call "Closed for renovations" They ended Evo and promised to come back with a great new design and wonderful new concept.

This is always the problem with new places, or old places getting the face lift with a little botox for good measure. The problem, the question that should be asked and I don't think is, is, do we really go to restaurants because of their concept? If we love Johnny Depp pirate flicks, are we more predisposed to love a new bistro called the Buccaneer, with their signature dish, the Walk the Plank Flank Steak? We can have a Sports Bar with a Difference, with a Point Break themed bar, it is surfing and football and Keanu. Doesn't everyone want to go that bar? Who doesn't love that movie? I mean you can have a 50 Year Wave Shooter.

All of this to say that the owners of Evo came back with the Bootleggers Prohibition Pub. That's right, its a prohibition themed bar restaurant. You remember that time? When people died from drinking wood alcohol. When people went blind or discovered their limbs shaking uncontrollably because of the bad booze they were pounding. When gangsters tightened their grip on city economies. Let's have a bar celebrating that.

I was given my 7.50 gin and tonic (Wednesday at 7:30) in a mason jar. Not a real mason jar, but a mass produced replica to give you that mass produced nostalgia. Here is Dave being an annoying effete. I don't want to drink a highball in a mason jar. I would like to have it in a highball glass. If I must, then a decent pint glass, or even a small snifter. Something that is kind and pleasant to the hand holding it. A mason jar is not fun to hold, it's kind of silly.

The drink was okay. It didn't make me blind. I didn't lose control of my legs. That's a good cocktail in a prohibition pub, right? Maybe that's why they called themselves a prohibition pub, to lower the bar on their cocktails. Continue to live = good cocktail. Dying in a fit = sub par cocktail. They should put that on their ad copy. "Come to the Bootleggers Prohibition Saloon -

Our Drinks Won't Kill Ya!"

The bar is now prominent, in the middle of the room. The tables are non-descript. There is sports on but one of the flat screens is showing an old movie playing on TCM. The idiot in me was annoyed that they weren't playing silent movies. It should be movies from the 20s. Could that be so hard?

The waitress was wearing a flapper dress. It was black and slinky and covered in tassels. I looked at that and I could imagine her leaning over at a table and a platoon of those tassels falling into the soup of the day.

It was quiet there on that Wednesday and it just felt forced.

A while back, I discovered a group of essays written in the New Yorker magazine during the 1920s about illegal bars. The series was Speakeasy Nights by Niven Busch. They were cute and funny at first, but as I continued to read them on the New Yorker online archive, I discovered that the stories were sad. The places described were run down and all the smiles and humor felt like a facade. It wasn't the writing. It was the places being written about. There was a desperation.

The speakeasy was a sad kind of thing. A placeholder. An illegal room, an apartment, an untidy flat. The liquor was poor and the food overpriced.

Is this what we want our new bars to emulate? A run down joint, two steps away from being busted? On their Facebook account, they sometimes inform you of special events and give the password. Passwords are a fun exclusive thing, but only if you want to go in.

2020 Update. It closed within a year of opening. The sign is still there. But the place is gone. I don't know what they are doing with the space, but it's not a restaurant anymore.

Letter 11 - Gin and Tonics at Scal's

Dear Worcester,

There is a corner in Worcester, that has an establishment that is always one of two things: a bar or an empty storefront that used to be a bar. In the 18 years I have been in the Worcester area, it has been a variety of bars. The corner is Mill Street and Main. You can find it in Webster Square. It used to Noamesco, Crow Bar, End Zone, and there were others. The names went fast and furious. I just spent a little time searching for those names and could not find them. That seems apt to me, the names of failed bars should not be kept forever on the internet. The names of failed bars should be forgotten like that fourth or was it that fifth shot of whisky. The names of failed bars should only be recalled in a restless sleep and then dissipate once more soon after waking.

A friend told me stories about going to that bar twenty years ago. Due to one of the stories, he and his workmates called the bar the Four Buck Pub. The story was so unsavory, I will not repeat it. Let us just say that you don't want to know what the four bucks paid for, and let's be pleased the establishment has changed hands. And changed hands. And changed hands.

It is now called Scal's. It just opened about a week ago. It had been closed for quite a few months and now once again it was a drinking establishment.

Another friend from Nick's took me aside the other day and whispered that she saw me coming out of the bar Scal's. "That place that's always some bar in Webster Square." I told her I was doing it for the gin and tonic tour and she felt a little better about the whole thing. She told me that it has been a bar forever, a bar she never felt the need to enter. She said it's not a great area and the parking is awful around there.

I told her that I read on the bar's Facebook that they arranged late night parking in the Chinese Restaurant across the street on Main. (See,

I do my homework.) We talked about the madness, the pure hubris, in expecting a bar to survive.

In town, a bar might run down to nothing and turn into a farm stand (like the Alibi) or be paved over for a highway like 146 (as in the case of the Irish Club). Some bars are just husks. Due to liens and restrictions, they are just skeletons, that remain and wither (Irish Times and others). These will never be bars again. They are just ghosts. Ghosts you walk by not noticing them. Only when you are thirsty and lonely does it appear on the side of your glance.

But this corner. This corner is but cursed to always rise again as another drinking parlor.

Doomed for eternity. The zombie apocalypse can sweep through the streets of Worcester, and this place will open up once more, serving the finest brain gin fizzes.

I went on a Sunday, in the middle of Memorial Day Weekend. I think I got there around seven or so. It looks better than it used to.

I had not been into the bar that is now Scal's for something like a decade. Maybe even longer.

The new owners definitely improved it. The bar is in the back. It's comfortable. There is a focus on sports on the flat screens and there is a pool table and an area for darts. About ten people were in there. The bartender didn't know what to do for a standard gin and tonic and he went to, what seemed to be the owner, who informed him that he toss in a little Tanquray with tonic and that will do the trick. It did. A fine drink for six bucks. No complaints there.

Actually, there will be no complaints at all. It's not fair. It's not fair to judge a bar on the first few days. Yes, the only people there were friends of the bar. They all knew each other. It did feel like a clubhouse with me elbowing in uninvited.

But it is brand new and it needs to build its brand. I hope that it will do well. I hope that it will thrive. But let me frank? Does Worcester need another joint with a dart board and a pool table? Is there too much of a log jam at the other 20 or so "sports bars" that there needs to be another? Do we require another flat screen laden wall showing Red Sox and ESPN 2? Do we need the same thing we have down the road, just in a cleaner, newer model?

I ask these questions not to be a jerk (being a jerk is just an added bonus) but because I really don't know. Is there an endless need for a good bar? Are our alcohol drenched shoulders large enough to carry all comers across the river to success?

I hope so. I have seen too many bars disappear. I am almost relieved that there is this corner, this bar phoenix. It is here as a sign that the bar scene is not going away. So you want a bar in Webster Square, this one ain't bad. Give it a try.

Until Next Time

Dave

Letter 12 - Gin and Tonics at Bahn Thai

Dear Worcester,

The drink tasted of ashes. I have had many gin and tonics in this seemingly endless tour of every bar in Worcester. I have had fine ones and forgettable ones and of course there were the poor excuses to the art of pouring booze in a glass. I have had countless gin and tonics, but this is the first one that tasted of arson.

In this lovely looking Thai restaurant, there is a sign, made on somebody's home inkjet printer, stating that they now have liquor. But they don't have a bar. They have what seemed to be a horseshoe seating, but now turned into a bar to accommodate the bottles nestled on a shelf by the wall. In the center of the horse shoe you can sit and act like you have sidled up to the stick. But there is only four chairs for that part and they were taken by a few Clark students. I sat on one of the sides, so the girl working the drinks detail walked to the other side of what was basically a table and got my drink order.

I don't know how long they had their liquor license, but she informed me that this was her first gin and tonic and that she hoped it was alright.

Let me stop here to state that I had my first gin and tonic when I was fourteen. My grandmother made it for me. Later on that summer, I was told that if I wanted a drink, I had to make my own. She tested the result for balance and potency, like every good grandmother does. In my career as a high school drinker, which is another way of saying a poor clueless drunk kid, I had experience making many cocktails. You pour the liquor in and then you pour in whatever is supposed to go with it, We never had tonic in our rumpus room bacchanales so we made do mixing our poor gin with Sprite. These drinks were not designed for or by discerning tastes, they were to cut the liquor enough to get it down. This is just to say that a two ingredient cocktail is something everyone should have mastered enough to not embarrass yourself when you find yourself working at a Thai restaurant on Park Avenue in Worcester.

The girl who concocted the drink was nice, and the place was nice. And everyone there on a Sunday night was nice, eating nice food.

The food was attractive, the spices permeated the whole joint. And I had an eight dollar and fifty cent glass of burnt offerings. In most cases, when a drink is this bad, I would not finish it. I tend to not complain about a bad drink, because let's be honest, when you are having an alcoholic beverage you are drinking poison.

But I found myself deliberately and slowly taking bites off of this cocktail. Not as a connoisseur of fine high balls, but as a crime scene investigator. "How did something so simple, so elegant, go so wrong?"

I tried to place the ashen flavor. Did I get the right liquor? Was this a new Polar flavor, Yesterday's Campfire Seltzer? Could there be something wrong with the dishwasher? Or is it me? Am I tasting things wrong, am I having a stroke?

The girl who made me the drink spent most of her time talking to two other young women at the "bar." They were having what looked like tasty food. They spoke about college and how hard it is to pay off tuition. I sat by myself. Lost in the Puzzle of the Ashen Highball (look at me, I turned my excursion into every bar in Worcester into a forgotten Sherlock Holmes mystery.) She came over to me and asked me how the drink was. She was very pleasant. I told her it was great. Just great. Yeah. Great. Let's call it great.

Some places shouldn't be bars. They should just serve good food. Isn't that hard enough? The place was handsome and the food smelled good. Shouldn't that amazing feat be enough for anyone? Can't we just look at how we don't even know how to create a bar area and throw in the towel? Can't we say, we are just not bar people. We are food people, let us celebrate that.

Bahn Thai is located at 2 Coes Square. Go there for the food and the pleasant service. When having a Pad Thai, do you really need a cocktail? Enjoy the flavor of the food. Let that be your highball.

Until Next Time

Dave

Letter 13 - Bars and Vibrations

Dear Worcester,

Today my son and I went to the TouchTomorrow program at WPI. It was lovely. We participated in science experiments, learned about the universe and watched robots attack Styrofoam noodles. It was a great time. They even had a Van de Graaff generator there, ready for the kids to touch and the parents to take photos destined to embarrass the child years later, during dating season no doubt. My son demurred. He didn't want to see his hair standing on end. I did. But that's a father for you.

My son wanted to eat and wanted to eat in air conditioning. I did a few calculations in my head and suggested we walk to the Boynton. My son, eight years old, loves places with grilled cheese sandwiches and fries. The Boynton has such a thing on the menu, so the kid loves the place.

Long time readers of these reports from the front might well remember that I don't care for the Boynton at all. It has never worked for me. I think it thinks too highly of itself. But it was nearby and the kid loves it. Who doesn't want to be the world's greatest dad? Or at least, passably acceptable dad? I'll take it.

It was pretty busy this afternoon, but I saw booths and tables. I asked for a table for two and the hostess took us to the bar area, to a booth in the front.

I wasn't going to ask for another booth, but I was already a little weary. If I was with friends and was seated there, great. But I had the kid, and that means I have to be concerned with the bar. The bar, as you know, is a place I love. There is drinking and swearing and lying. Three things I don't allow my son to do.

I have been at bars at 2pm on a Saturday where it sounds like an amateur hour production of Reservoir Dogs.

Kids in the bar area is never a groovy concept. Am I, the parent, expecting everyone to curb their behavior? No. A bar should be a bar. An animal preserve for base behavior. I don't want to be "That Guy" who wants you to be polite because there are children present. On the other hand, I really don't want people to be going on about the "fucking" Red Sox and their "fucking" manager.

Part of me was annoyed. Didn't the hostess see me with a kid? Couldn't she have put me in one of the non-bar areas. But the hostess has to be fair to the wait staff. If the waitress in the bar area is up for the next party, then she will get the next group, even if you are putting an eight year old in the bar area of a busy restaurant when you don't have to

I understand that getting as many tables as possible is important for wait staff, but I don't know. This is a relationship, the wait staff and the customer. Shouldn't both sides be considered?

We ordered our drinks and then my son looked at me seriously. "Daddy. Is it okay if we switch seats."

And like that, I am in over protective father mode. "Sure buddy. Why? Is something wrong? Are you seeing something bad?"

He looked confused at the question. "No Daddy. Everything is alright. It's just that, the seat is vibrating and it's very distracting."

Vibrating booth seats? Ooooo-kay. Someone walked around in the sun for a little too long? Someone needs a nap, and why don't kids his age take naps? Naps would solve so many issues. "Sure, no problem. Let's switch."

So I sat down and got comfortable, and. And. There it was. The seat was vibrating. It wasn't throwing me from the seat like I was at a Gilley's mechanical bull, but no doubt about it, the damned seat was vibrating. Hell, maybe I need a nap.

I got the eye of a waiter passing by, not ours, and said, a little embarrassed to do it, "Uhm, it seems that the seat is vibrating."

The guy nodded, "Yeah. The beer cooler is underneath that seat and so it vibrates. There is nothing we can do about it." Nothing to do about it? How about not have a seating over the vibrating beer cooler. But I didn't say that. I asked to get another seat and we did,

I was annoyed enough to ask our new waitress why they would seat people in a sub par location when they don't have to. She looked glassy at me and apologized and then asked what we would have for lunch.

So perhaps I should not have asked the waitress this question, so I will ask you, here in this forum. You have a table with a seat that vibrates, do you sit people and hope they don't mention it, or do you not sit people there? Is the important thing shoving in as many people in, or creating a positive experience?

Of course, a vibrating seat might be a positive experience for some people.Do people slip the hostess a fin to get seated at the vibrating booth? Is it the talk of the underground diners of Central Massachusetts? "The food is mediocre, but you will have the most relaxed lower back you ever had. Come for the vibrating booths, stay for the chicken wings

I know this is not really about bars, and definitely not about gin and tonics, but its a restaurant with a bar and I am just curious. I am curious about who is the important member in the bar-customer relationship. The customer is not always right. But should the restaurant also treat them like an inconvenience? We have a vibrating booth, well they will just have to suck it up if they want to be here. That's not what they are thinking, but it's a little bit how they are presenting themselves.

Let's make this a thing. I will be tickled if people go to the Boynton and ask for the booth with the vibrating seat, the Good Vibrations Seat. Wouldn't that be lovely. And let's see how they respond to the wants and desires of their customers.

Until Next Time

Dave

Letter 14 - Bars and Research

Dear Worcester,

I thought I would show with you how I conduct research for this collection of letters. There is the drinking of gin and tonics at the bars of Worcester, of course. Then, there is the discussion I have afterwards. I have a little group I bounce ideas off and I air questions about the things that puzzled me at the bars.

The discussions take place at a bar. I was with a friend and a bartender (who is also a friend, but for this letter, they will be called Friend and Bartender, got it? These things should include a dramatis personae in the first paragraph of every post). I got my beer and was asked if I had been to any bars and like that, the brain trust was called into order.

"Okay, here's something that happened at the latest bar," I said to the bartender. "I got a gin and tonic that was eight bucks and forty two cents. I gave a twenty. The bartender brought back eleven dollars."

"Wait," my friend said, "where was the change, the 58 cents?"

"That's the thing," I said. "It wasn't there. He didn't give me the change. Just the eleven dollars. But he also gave me the receipt and it said 8.42. I am only talking about half a buck here. Is that a thing? Take the change as a service charge?"

The Bartender was savvy and quickly said, "Don't write it. Don't include that in your blog. That was just a mistake. Was it busy?"

"Yeah, there were people and things were moving along."

"There you go," the Bartender said. "This was just a mistake he made. He didn't mean to do it. Because why would he blow the chance for a 1.50 tip just by taking fifty cents? I mean, there was a chance when you noticed he shorted you, you were not going to give him anymore tip, right?"

"I thought about it."

"And if he knew that, why would he chance that? You might not throw that dollar or even more. Why? Just to take fifty cents? Believe me, it was just a mistake. Don't write it." There is something endearing about witnessing a bartender protecting one of his brethren. I agreed, but said I might write about it without names.

"Since we're talking about weird bartender behavior I got a question about a waiter," my Friend said, "I was at an Italian joint with a date. I had an appetizer, ate it with a fork. The fork was on the plate when I finished with it. The waiter came over put down my entree. Instead of giving me a new fork, he picked up the one on the appetizer plate and he didn't put it next to the plate, he placed it right into my entree. Weird right?"

"I never would do that," the Bartender said. "I will ask if they want a new fork. Always. And I wouldn't put it in the food. That's not right. It's fine to use the same utensil, but you ask if they are good with that."

"That's what I thought," my Friend said.

The Bartender went to take care of a few customers and came back when he could. "Last night was one of those nights. Crazy customers who don't know how to behave in a bar. I had this one girl come in with some friends and she just said, 'I want something blue." That's all she could identify. Something blue. I tried to be helpful. I asked her what things she likes. She said she wanted something blue. Blue is not a flavor. It is a color. You don't drink colors. Her friend had a mojito and the girl said that that looked yummy. I told her I could make a blue mojito by putting in blue curacao. She said no. She wanted something blue. I told her I could make a blue margarita. She asked me what went in that and I told her. She said that sounds great and I made it for her. She hated it. And I charged her the full amount. There are no discounts for ordering a blue drink and not liking it."

There were more conversations and revelations as the evening went on. But that's a bar for you. And that is how I do research for these academic entries.

Until Next Time

Dante

Letter 15 - Gin and Tonics at Livia's Dish

Dear Worcester

I went to a place I couldn't get to during the original tour two years ago. This place was Livia's Dish. I heard they had a full bar but the dinner time ended quickly and I couldn't get to it before it closed, so I gave it up for too much work. I mean, I ain't paid for this. Hell, I am paying for the right of creating these letters. One cocktail at a time. This is the kind of thing that professional writers shun: do not pay for the permission to be a writer. They also say: don't drink too much or you will turn into a writerly cliche. Well, looks like I'm batting a thousand on what not to do.

Today, because I knew I was leaving work early and had no commitments, I looked up places I might go to. I checked out Livia's Dish and read that they are now a brunch only place. They go to three every day of the week. And yes, they still have a full bar. Of course they do. How else could they make the necessary mimosas? I figured I could get there by two and why not? Let's try another gin and tonic and another place I have never been. It's pure evolutionary science. Man comes out of the muck, then man makes ridiculous goal that revolves around alcohol.

I got there and it was a very nice looking place. There is a ground floor and then quickly steps going to a second level where there is a bar and additional tables. Guess where I went?

The place was winding down. There were two parties at tables, finishing off, talking and lingering. I was by myself at the five seat bar. It was wide and presentable. There was a flatscreen showing a cooking show. The waitress slash bartender gave me a menu and greeted me warmly. Now, my problem was, this was a brunch place. At no time does it feel like the kind of place you walk into just for a cocktail. That's just strange. So I decided to order something for lunch. This violated my rule, but I didn't know who to avoid it.

Scanning the menu, I knew I wanted a salad. But first. I ordered the item that brought me here in the first place: a gin and tonic. It was almost a treat that the woman didn't ask me what kind of gin. All they had was Tanqueray and Tanqueray was what I was to have. There is a pleasant sensation in surrendering decisions to the bartender. "Just make it."

The drink came for seven dollars and I took a sip of it before I ordered my food. It was a nice cocktail. I liked it. Maybe not top ten gin and tonics in this tour, but hey, I would not spit this out with disgust. Sometimes you want a cocktail to taste like the cocktail always has, and this was it. You want a decent gin and tonic. This was it. And dealing with the vagaries of cocktail manufacturing in this day and age, getting a decent cocktail is a beautiful thing. This is just me saying, if you need to go to a brunch place and have a drink, then you can order a gin and tonic here and you will be pleased.

Then I ordered a salad and she told me that the pecans that are supposed to be in the salad are not available and they will have walnuts instead. I am allergic to walnuts and I am sad to report I felt a little put out. Not for anything they did, people run out of pecans, it happens, but because I was pissed that I have this annoying allergy. So I looked at my choices and said, "You know what, I am cool, I will stick with the gin and tonic, thanks."

This was kind of a relief. It meant I could continue with just having a drink and no food for this tour. The bartender apologized a few times, but I was happy and told her so. I said a gin and tonic is three or four tiers of the nutritional pyramid.

Behind me, a group of dentists were telling horror stories of the trade. They had just come in from playing golf. Another couple was in the front room. The two waitresses and I were in the bar watching the mid-day news. The weatherman was wearing a buttoned sports coat that didn't fit him. It strained against his belly. "There are scores of people around him, why wouldn't someone tell him to unbutton that thing. Or get a jacket that fits." I said.

The bartender said, "Yeah, he has put on some weight. Why wouldn't someone say that that is not a good look."

The other waitress said, "Of course the weather women don't have that problem. They are all so thin and wearing dresses that show off too much. None of them should be bending down too quickly."

"But what is it," the bartender said, "with them? Even the ones not in good shape, they all have really toned arms. Every weather woman has these sculpted arms. Like they are doing curls with weights before each time they go on air."

The conversation went on. We talked about weather people and weather and that this is a nice place to work at. "Not too many people here right now though," I said.

The bartender said, "It's after two in the afternoon, we close at three. It's the end of the night for us. Last call."

Nothing important was said in this conversation. No one opened their souls. No one learned something important. Life lessons were not on the menu. But everyone had a nice moment chatting, killing time, enjoying the end of the night - in the middle of the afternoon.

The thing about what I do, is that it is not a comprehensive review of a place. But I get an impression. I really liked being at Livia's Dish. The place was bright and inviting. The staff was terrific. The food looked good and they made a fine gin and tonic. I will definitely try out the brunch with my family soon.

It is always fun to talk smack about a place, but it is more satisfying to speak well of a restaurant.

Until Next Time

Dave

Letter Sixteen - Bars and Endings

Dear Worcester

For over three years or so, I have been going to the bars and restaurants of Worcester, ordering a gin and tonic, drinking it, leaving the place soon after and writing about it in a blog whimsically titled Gin and Tonics Across Worcester. I did 144 bars and restaurants in eighteen months and then called myself done with the silly concept. Eight months later, in March of 2016 I decided to try a few more, the new places, and the blog started again. I wrote about 15 new places. Then I stopped again. March showed up in 2017 and I decided to do it one more time. This time in the form of letters. I wrote about gin and tonic, but I allowed myself the right to go on about bars and those who have an affinity for just such a place.

I really enjoyed this format and was invigorated by the process once more. I wrote over a dozen of these letters by the end of June 2017. I went to two more places for gin and tonics: Valentino's and The Fix. I made a list of a handful of new places and a list of places that were to open sometime in the year that I planned to visit.

Then I stopped.

During the summer, I was working on longer writing projects and completely forgot about the quest for bars and gin and tonic. By the end of the summer, when I did recall the blog, I could not find the energy nor drive to jump start it.

Also, I wasn't drinking much. My acid reflux didn't care for my alcohol consumption. I had to cut back. I was going to Nick's occasionally, but I didn't have the desire to drink as an act of discovery. I didn't have the time or the inclination to schlep myself to a new unknown bar and write about the experience. Maybe this was me getting old and set in my ways. Is that really so bad?

This blog helped me be more consistent with writing, but now I wanted to write about other things. I have one book available as an ebook and others ready to be copyedited and formatted to be self published. That's where the focus has turned.

I still love writing about bars. I still love going to bars, or at least my regular bar, but I am quite done with having a gin and tonic in every bar in Worcester. It was a wonderful fancy that propelled me through over three years and a hundred thousand words. I do have a few ideas about writing about bars and drinkers but I need to finish a few other things first.

I was going to just leave the blog and the project unfinished. But I began to assemble these letters and some of the older posts into a book and I realized that I needed to write one final letter explaining why I have stopped. Of course, it is this letter.

I needed to say goodbye.

I needed to say thank you.

I began this project to discover why people go to bars. Why you decide to pick a place and drink in public. I never came up with an answer, but I was blessed with an opportunity to know my city in an intimate fashion. I am blessed by this project. I have seen so many parts of our community and I am really grateful.

I want to thank all of you who stuck with me during these posts. I want to thank those who commented and those who disagreed. I want to thank my friends for putting up with this and for those who helped me with information and advice.

Gin and Tonics Across Worcester does not have to be done. It is just me that is done. If anyone else wants to discover the bars and joints of Worcester by having one cocktail at each place, please, enjoy the tour. I know I did.

Here's a toast to you. The Reader. And to you. Worcester.

Yours,

David

Appendix One - Earlier Posts

That should be enough, but there is enough thoughts and experiences about Worcester bars that I like to share a few more pieces from you. These are all posts written before the third iteration, when I wrote the letters. These were all from the second go round from me.

Wicked Wings Company (Posted May 2016)

The chalkboard in the front of the place thanks their customers in voting them the best new restaurant in Worcester.

It is Friday at eight and it is mostly full. I get the last seat at the bar.

It is quiet for such a full place. The Sox game is on, but no music is playing. People are speaking in muted tones, as if this was a church with Jalapeno Buffalo sauce.

The gin and tonic is five dollars and thirty five cents and it tastes of syrup. It is alright. Alright, like getting out of the Registry of Motor Vehicles office in under an hour. That kind of alright.

Large platters of wings dressed in different colored sauces are paraded out to the tables.

I am trying to wonder why I feel so unengaged. It is Friday. There are wings. There is beer. Where is the joy? I check the menu, both sides. No joy.

I get it.

The bartenders, two women moving and shaking and stirring, do not smile. They have stony faces. They are concentrating for the exam. They are waiting in line at the Registry. They are anywhere but at a fun place to be.

I look and the other staff also have that same serious face. Buffalo wings is serious business.

I realize that at any bar, I want the bartender to be happy to be here. I don't need a flirty bartender, or my next best friend bartender. Just some one who seems pleased that they are here surrounded by alcohol and people. And pleased that I am one of them.

As I leave, I see one of the bartenders smile for a regular. It's nice that she can. Maybe I need to be here for four weeks in a row before I earn a smirk. Things to aspire to.

I am sure the wings are good. Why wouldn't they be?
The Wicked Wing Co is located at 321 West Boylston Street.

A Tale of Three Whiskeys (Posted June 2016)

Chapter One: The Gin and Tonic meets Whiskey

This is going to be a long piece of reporting. Longer than most. I know that you all check in on this blog to get hard hitting investigative journalism. To get to the heart of the gin and tonic crisis in Worcester bars.

No. You check in because I created a very silly goal for myself. To go to every bar in Worcester and order and drink a gin and tonic. Some people donate their time to running food banks. I give back to the community by drinking at a lot of different places.

I did it faithfully for eighteen or so months, writing up 144 bars and the gin and tonics I encountered. It was great. I stopped it and then six months later I decided that I wanted to check out the bars I didn't get to. The new ones, the ones I was too fatigued to do during the first time.

This was in March (three months ago) and I posted that I was to start and that very week I gave myself a Friday night to hit three new bars. They had something in common and I thought grouping them together was a fine idea.

Then I just didn't write them up. I forgot when I did the blog, that the going to the bars was easy. Writing about them was not. When I did the blog originally, I was very structured on how to write them. On starting up again, I wanted to free the writing form from how I did it. But I couldn't get it to work.

So a month later I went to another new bar and just started there. Ignoring those three bars. I don't even know if those bars are still open or if they are still behaving the same way that I saw them. I don't know, and for this exercise in completeness, I don't care. .

The three bars I went to all had the same word in their name and I couldn't resist not going to them all in one go.

The word is "whiskey."

Chapter Two: The Word on Everyone's Lips is Whiskey

Naming your bar after a type of spirit or cocktail is courting ruin.

What if you are named Side Car Saloon and your side car is sub par? How will your customers feel if you can't deliver what's in your name? You're called the Side Car, and this is no respectable side car. Good day sir!

In my initial tour of the bars of Worcester, I went to two places named after drinks: Sake Bomb and Mai Tai. I didn't see anyone drink a sake bomb at said location, but my opinion is that you shouldn't set yourself up by having the word bomb in your name. "Sake is not the only thing to bomb here." I had very bad service there, so I felt like it did bomb for me.

At Mai Tai, I did see the eponymous drink made. From pre made ingredients living in a plastic bottle at the well of the bar. That place felt prefabricated as well. From the Asian-Restaurant-Bar-Popular-With-The-Kids kit that you order from the back of a comic book. Some assembly required.

In those 144 bars, none of them had the word Whiskey in the name. Not one.

Then I take a hiatus for six months and we suddenly get Whiskey (a bar on Main Street), Whiskey Tango (on Park Avenue) and Whiskey on Water (which is on Water Street, natch).

Is there any reason why, out of the very veil of nothingness, Worcester has been suddenly graced with three bars all with pretty much the same name?

Why whiskey? Is it the hot new alcoholic thing? Like Zima?

Did three enterprising bar owners all lose bets?

Why not another alcoholic mainstay? Couldn't we have three bars all names Vodka? Martini is a good name for a bunch of bars. How bout a string of roadside dives all named Hooch (which could mean either blinding cheap liquor or the beloved movie dog).

Chapter Three: What's in a Name?

When I say a bar is named Whiskey, do you not think then that it is a whiskey bar? I do. So the question then is, what is a whiskey bar?

Let me hazard an uninformed opinion (as all my opinions are).

The bar is tony, with hardwood, comfortable chairs and stools. If one could smoke there would be ornamental ash trays ready to take any stogie. There would be a menu of opulently priced examples and fine glasses to drink them in. The conversation is muted and I imagine jazz being played.

Let me put it another way, a whiskey bar is the kind of place a Bond villain drinks at.

That's what you imagine. Not just me. When I told people I went to three bars named Whiskey everyone asked about them in regard to it being a place where you can drink expensive liquors in a comfortable environment.

And I then I said, "No, none of them were whiskey bars. Not a one."

Chapter Four: How the Evening Went (an Overview)

At a little after nine in the evening I went to Whiskey, which is on Main Street. I was there for no more than ten minutes.I was the only person in the bar. I then arrived at Whiskey Tango on Park Avenue at 9:35 where I was the only person in the bar. I talked to the bartender for forty minutes or so. It was after ten when I made it to Whiskey on Water, on Water Street. It was busy in there and getting more packed by the minute. They were setting up the velvet rope outside when I left twenty minutes later.

Only Whiskey on Water had a whiskey menu. But no one I saw was drinking one, and I was looking. The bartender from Whiskey Tango and I were talking about whiskey bars and he was dismissive about Whiskey on Water. The story he told was a friend of his, who loves good scotch, went as soon as Whiskey on Water opened and got the pretty bartender's attention and asked her some detailed questions about the whiskey they had. She rolled her eyes, gave him the menu and said, "Just look at the menu." She then turned and left him. He left the bar without ordering.

This is just the story from a guy working at a rival bar with Whiskey in its name. But my impression of Whiskey on Water allows me to believe it.

So the thing they all three had in common was that none of them were whiskey bars and the plastic cups.

Chapter Five: The Common Denominator (the Cups)

All three of the bars with whiskey in the name served me my (not inexpensive) gin and tonics in plastic cups. All three. I was beginning to wonder if the bartenders were calling ahead and telling the next stop I was coming and I was not deserving of glassware.

Going through my notes of the first 144 bars, I can only find four bars where I was served in plastic cups: Cisero's, , Pleasant Cafe, City Lights and Azteca. The rates of plastic cup appearances are very low. But then I come back and hit three in a row and get my seven dollar drink in a plastic cup.

If this sounds like I am being a snob, then you have been paying attention. I am being a snob. Listen, I have gone to 150 plus bars and in most cases have had subpar gin and tonics, the least I want is a comfortable, solid piece of glass to hold onto. Like an anchor.

Also, the plastic cup can tell you a little bit about the place. Dive bar. College bar. Bar where they don't know any better. What is this thing called a dishwasher?

Chapter Six: What is the Proper Hunting Season for Bars?

For those that have read this blog, you know that I have been dogged by the fact that I can't seem to get to a bar when it is busy and full of its proper element.

This is me. I have a family and going out at ten on Friday or Saturday is not something I can swing often. I would go in the middle of the day, on a Sunday perhaps. Or Wednesdays or other times when the hunting is thin.

My response was always, you go to 144 bars. You see if you can swing prime bar time for all of them. And when is that really? I remember going to one bar and they said that every other Thursday is the time to be there, every other Thursday when they have the karaoke machine going. That's when I should be there. Mark you calendar.

The truth is, every bar is an odd eco system where only luck, and knowledge will allow you to discover when the good times are.

Or maybe the bar is just a raft on a large sea, floating far away from any known shipping lanes and it is only just some time before the next big storm will topple it over.

Chapter Seven: The First Bar Named Whiskey

It tries mightily to look like a whiskey bar, but the place is more open than I would expect. Maybe I think that because it is empty.

I sit at the bar. The girl behind the bar gives me my plastic cup. She is setting up for the night when people might show up to go crazy. The bar manager is there asking the girl where the other bartender is, shouldn't she be here already? She gives an excuse or two and the bar manager doesn't believe it.

The drink is seven dollars and alright at best. The emptiness of the place is exhausting.

I look and the bar has a small shelf of high end whiskeys but that is clearly ornamental. On either side of the bar are sets of spirits but on inspection, each side has the same spirits, so the selection looks big, but is pretty small.

I ask the bartender when it gets busy, she says at eleven or later, it can get pretty crazy.

There is something off about a place that only is alive for a few hours a week. With some places you can tell its going to get busy and alive later, I felt this place was questionable. Maybe people will come. Maybe.

The bartender said to me, "Sorry, you came too early, you missed all the craziness." Thanks, I will be fine.

Chapter Eight: The Second Bar Named Whiskey (Whiskey Tango)

No one but me and the bartender. Great, another bust. It had no special whiskeys. Just a name that was more about some vague military fetish than a desire for fine spirits. The place used to be Nuff Sed, and then it was Micky O'Neil's and now it was Whiskey Tango and it looked exactly the same as the last iteration. The gin and tonic was six bucks in a plastic cup and the plastic improved the flavor.

Luckily, the bartender, who told me he was the bar manager, liked my Star Wars tee shirt and we chatted for a while. I got the skinny.

The bar started up with the plan of being a high end location for good spirits and wines. That didn't happen. If people were coming in, they weren't coming in for high end wines. As a matter of fact, most days were as anemic as this night. Then they hired this kid from Worcester State to tend bar and like magic, Whiskey Tango became a Worcester State Bar.

The issue is, when you are a Worcester State Bar, you are full of life and excitement...for seven and half hours a week. Thursday thru Saturday from eleven to one thirty. There is no whiskey drinking, but a lot of beer. The place is hopping, but at all other times it is empty.

The bar manager told me tales of other bars and living the bartender life. They were fun to hear. I wished him well and after forty five minutes I figured it was time for me to move on.

Two months later, I went to the new restaurant Dead Horse Hill, and that same bartender was there. He told me he moved on. Whiskey Tango still had no action. He was happier at the new place.

As I said earlier, I really don't know if it is still in business. Now that Worcester State is mostly empty with summer vacation, who knows who will come. That stretch of Park Avenue is known for hosting college bars. Its nice that someone was trying to create something new, but what if your potential customer base will not accept change?

There is something to be said for a quiet nearly empty bar, it can be fun. But not all the time.

Chapter Nine: We Finally Get to Whiskey on Water

When I first heard of Whiskey on Water, the article mentioned that the concept was to have food trucks in the back parking lot and you can use an app to order food and it will be delivered to you. Some friends think that's an awesome idea. I don't know if that really happens. I didn't see anyone with food. I just saw beer and fruity happy drinks.

Whiskey on Water is a very popular place. Scores of people were there and more were coming. Women out for a night. Guys ready to try to get some action from said groups of women. The second floor was a dance floor. Too early for dancing, so a lot of High School Gym dance behavior with people congregating on the edges, waiting for critical mass for the boogying to explode.

There is nothing wrong with this type of place. It's not the kind of place I like. There is definitely a need for a dance club, because people were lining up and excited to come.

The bar is beautiful and has lovely bottles. Bottles guarded by bartenders who are more intent on looking fine and pouring Budweiser.

My one complaint was watching the men my age sitting at the bar wolf eyeing all the young women. I guess that's part of the deal, but ick.

On the ground floor, a woman was singing popular hits, accompanied by a thing young dude with a guitar. She said she got a request for a song she didn't know, so she sang it while reading the lyrics on her phone.

The gin and tonic was seven dollars and it was actually a very nice drink.

Fifteen minutes

And then, the night of bars with whiskey in their names was over.

Chapter Ten: All Good Things

So that's it. I spent a little over seventy five minutes in three bars three months ago and I have now spent four hours writing about it. I couldn't find a way to write this. I am not sure if I wrote about it well here, but at least it is written.

Maybe my issue is that these three bars named whiskey really solidified my feeling on finding the right bar in Worcester. Two places were completely empty, but in one I had a great conversation. The guy who I had the nice talk with isn't there anymore, so why go? The last place was packed and I was completely not where I would like to be. The last place was alive and crazy and thumping and in two years it will probably be empty with the owners by themselves drinking cocktails from plastic cups, wondering why they were forsaken for the next thing, the next big bar with Whiskey in its name.

Whiskey is located at 316 Main Street

Whiskey Tango is located at 377 Park Avenue

Whiskey on Water is located at 97 Water Street

2020 Update: *Whiskey Tango is now a pretty nice coffee shop. As far as I know, the other two are still open and thriving.*

The Oaken Barrel (Posted July, 2016)

I went to the Oak Barrel Tavern for a gin and tonic. It's what I do.

This used to be Tweed's, which I thought was old looking and dull when I visited a few years back. This new version is very whiskey bar and modern restaurant. It had a nice neo bistro feel. The bar was made from strong wood slats, it was nice. The selection of whiskeys was impressive.

It was a Sunday night around eight thirty or so. They had three bartenders working, which felt like overkill, but it's a new place and things will settle I suppose. I didn't further my investigation but it looked like one of the bartenders was the same guy who served me back when it was Tweed's. I don't know for certain, but it looked like that. The more things change....

The gin and tonic was given and I paid 7.49 (I think, it was two weeks ago and I can't recall completely) and it was an alright glass, nothing fantastic, but serviceable.

But that's not what I came to talk to you about.

What I want I talk about is control. More precisely, who is control of a bar? The bartender or the patrons? Who makes the bar what it is?

When I entered, there were three women at the end of the bar drinking and eating and cussing. Cussing a lot. They spoke loudly and the word fuck was in every sentence, because hey sunshine, this is Worcester and this is how we talk.

Wait, sorry. Got that wrong.

This is fucking Worcester and this is how we fucking talk.

There, that's Worcester.

One of the women in the swearing bacchanale had her nine year old child with her, who was wandering around the tables, looking bored.

One of the women said, "Yeah, I can fuck that shit up. I can fuck that shit up." It's a good thing she only said that mantra twice, because at three times, the Candy Man comes out of the mirror and really fucks shit up.

The swearing and the shouting at this restaurant/bar continued until the women decided it was fucking time to fucking go. And with their departure, the peaceful silence of redemption settled upon the room.

This is not a dive bar. This is not a sports bar where the Patriots are being routed by the Broncos and we have to swear at the TV.. It's a pseudo whiskey bar with a fine food menu. Actually, when I was at the scariest bar in the city last year, there was no swearing at all, everyone was too broken to form the words.

I was talking to Bartender Brian the week after I went to the Oak Barrel and told him about the swearing and the kid running around and he said, "That's the problem with a lot of bartenders. They have no control. You have to have control. You can't have them shouting and swearing, you can't have them screaming into their cell phone. If you don't have control, then you give it to the patrons and the place goes to hell. You don't have to be an asshole to have control, but you got to be the one running the place. You are the bartender, you tend, you run the bar. I'm sure they will say I'm suppressing their first amendment rights. Nothing in the First Amendment says you can be a rude asshole."

So is the issue with the bartenders or with the patrons. It's a new place, do they feel they can possibly alienate the clientelle by asking them not say fuck at the top of their lungs? If we don't let them swear then they won't come back. I am just a pourer of beer, how can I ask the kind people of Worcester to not scream fuck?

I wish them luck. The place looks great, filled with strong wooden bones. Let's hope the staff grows bones and spines as strong as the bar they stand behind.

The Oak Barrel Saloon is located at 229 Grove Street.

Appendix 2 - The Case of Brook's

When I did the first version of this blog, I almost stopped before I got going after the tenth bar. That was on May 11, 2014. That was Brook's. Let me reprint what I wrote from the previous book.

The Bar: Brook's

The Address 245 Lincoln Street

The Day and the Time Sunday at five, this was Mother's Day

The price I can't remember and can't find my notes, but I think it was five bucks.

Did they ask me if I wanted a lime Yes

What was the type of gin It was bar gin.

What was the gin and tonic like I must say, up until "The Incident" everything about the place was good and enjoyable. The drink was a pint glass number and it was good, it was not going to get mentioned in the gin section of the Wine Spectator, but it was nice company

The Joint They had stools outside by the front door so people can smoke while seated. It's a kind flourish I am sure. Going in, the carpet was dingy and the place still smelled of every cigarette ever smoked in the place. It was ingrained in the very wood. There was a long bar on one side where everyone was. The bar was pretty well crowded, which is nice to see. There was a low wall that divided the joint, the other side was where one played pool and darts, though no one was there. They were all drinking and talking. This was neighborhood bar all over. Everyone knew everyone else. Some were talking loud and joshing with the bartender. A couple guys would go over from time to time to the darts area to talk private like.

General Impressions Before "The Incident" I was composing in my head a pretty positive dispatch for this stop on the tour. I was composing in my head how every neighborhood needed a place to feel like you are part of the crowd. Early on a Sunday and everyone was just doing their thing. It was nice.

And then......

The guy, who was talking to a lot of folk, came up to where I was standing by myself, minding my own business. He walked up to me full, so I couldn't miss him. "Hi," he said his name and put out his hand. I told him my name (I didn't say Dante, for those who are interested) and took his hand. He didn't shake it as much as imitated a pneumatic press. He smiled at me, but the smile didn't get up to his eyes, ya know. "First time here." I said it was. "What brings you here." Now there are a lot of things I could have said, like "I'm a narc on duty" or "I go to bar to bar in town and have a gin and tonic and write about it" which are great ways to shorten my lifespan. Instead I said, "I was just driving by and saw the place and figured to have a drink." The guy never stopped staring at me, he nodded with that smile and said "Yeah, this is a good place for that." Its amazing all the things he told me that were not included in his words. Like, I don't know you and I don't like that and I got me a strong grip if you didn't notice before. What are you going to do about it.

He walked away from me, giving me the illusion of choice in the matter. I got the hell out of there. I didn't leave, I retreated.

Now I could be wrong, he could have just been friendly. But, I'm not wrong. Since then I have been more careful on where my eyes are while I have my gin and tonic, but man, what a welcome. Sometimes a neighborhood bar is for whom the bar considers to be neighbors, so be careful how you look and present yourself.

Amount of Time in the Joint 10 minutes

Will I come back No thanks. I don't know who my welcome wagon friend was, if he is there all the time, but I don't need the apparent risk. I was more welcome at Pleasant Cafe than here.

This was hard to write, and that sense of threat almost made me end this little project right there, but I am glad I continued.

End of the report.

Okay, are we caught up?

Last month, I finally finished the task of compiling for e-book, the first volume of Gin and Tonics Across Worcester. It took months to get it ready. I put it out and then last week, I discovered this book on my drive. I must have assembled it from the essays a few years ago and then completely forgot that I did it. This made getting it ready a pleasant activity.

So it is a coincidence that I get a comment on the blog. Since the blog is moribund, I don't get a lot of comments on it. The last one was six months ago telling me that I am a snob and bar owners don't care what I think. Then I got one today. It is from Chuck and I will share it below.

"I was a bartender at this gin joint. Not on the afternoon of your visit but I knew all the regulars. Before it closed December 31, 2019 I used to share your article about "Brooks" Pub with patrons. It never failed to get an "almost fell off the stool" belly laugh from the regulars. I attribute that to your excellent prose and to the fact they immediately recognized who greeted you during the "incident". He's actually a good person who would do you no harm. However in his (booze-enhanced?) zeal to look out for the neighborhood, he did not give you a proper welcome. It pains me to know you almost gave up this project because of his actions."

That little post made my day. It also allowed me to think differently from my first impression. That's the thing with this book and the previous one: it is all just first impressions. There is no real knowledge. Could it be that some of the bars I said were great places were in fact lousy? Sure. And the same could be said about Brook's. I hated my little trip there. It started good and then went to shit.

Could I be wrong about the guy, like Chuck claims. Possibly. Was he really just a friendly guy who was too eager because of drink? Maybe. But then, his drunk happy self comes across as second tier wise guy. I felt someone was trying to intimidate me, and I will stand by that.

With that said, I feel bad that Brook's closed. It was a neighborhood bar and that's a wonderful creation. The people from nearby have a place that is theirs. And now that is gone and probably not to be replaced.

Since I started this thing six years ago, a lot of bars closed, a lot of bars opened. But the comfy neighborhood bar? When those close, they are gone.

People will miss it. That little note from Chuck tells volumes of what a community can be. That they could recognize who I meant. That they found the whole thing funny. That they knew where they were going to be Friday night, or Sunday afternoon.

Maybe that one moment I was there was the bad moment. I got the wrong impression and let the blogging world know about my wrong impression. Maybe I spun it the wrong way.

But really, that's how impressions work. We base whether we like something or not in a split second. I went into a bunch of places and decided in a snap whether it was good or not.

That's not how we pick a bar. It could be close to our apartment. Our friend hangs out there. The bartenders are good to look at. The beer is cold. The gin and tonic is perfectly made.

Loving a bar might be instantaneous or it might take some time to notice its merits, its good side.

I leave it to you. Enjoy the journey. Be happy with whatever barstool you decide to call your own.

David

About the Book

Do you like bars? Do you like getting the same drink at every bar you go into? Well, Dave does. He spent several years going into every bar in Worcester and having a gin and tonic. He wrote about it in a blog. That became Gin and Tonics Across Worcester: The Book. It wasn't just about the gin and tonic, though it was pretty damned important. It was about why people go to bars. Why does someone pick one bar to be theirs?

After the initial run, Dave went back to write about some of the bars he missed. These are the letters he wrote. These are the dispatches from the trenches in the war of drinking in New England. The letters do go through the bars and what was good, what was bad, and what was just odd. They also look into the world of bar going. Does drinking and poetry mix? Should you date someone from your bar? What do you do if the bartender doesn't give you your change? Should kids be in bars? World beating questions. And we have answers, just as hard hitting.

Come back with Dave as he reports upon the front. They are funny, snarky and sometimes sad. Sit down. Get a beverage. It's always best to be hydrated before reading.

About the Author

David Macpherson is the author of a score of e-books. He has written about bars (Gin and Tonics Across Worcester), art galleries (Art in New England with Sid and Manny), cartoons (Mama Cass's Golden Caramel Bar), famous illustrators (I Kind of Knew Edward Gorey), obscure German science fiction (Are Your a True Life Form?) and many others.